Lerner SPORTS

NETHERLANDS NATIONAL SOCCER TEAMS

ULTIMATE FAN GUIDE

JANIE SCHEFFER

Lerner Publications ◆ Minneapolis

To Dad and Katie—you will always be my Pelé and Mia Hamm.

Lerner Publications Company
An imprint of Lerner Publishing Group, Inc.
241 First Avenue North
Minneapolis, MN 55401 USA

For reading levels and more information, look up this title at www.lernerbooks.com.

Main body text set in Aptifer Slab LT Pro.
Typeface provided by Linotype AG.

Editor: Evan Villas **Designer:** Viet Chu
Lerner team: Martha Kranes, Sue Marquis

Library of Congress Cataloging-in-Publication Data

Names: Scheffer, Janie, 1992– author
Title: Netherlands national soccer teams : ultimate fan guide / Janie Scheffer.
Description: Minneapolis : Lerner Publications, [2026] | Series: Lerner Sports. World Cup fan guides | Includes bibliographical references and index. | Audience: Ages 7–11 | Audience: Grades 4–6 | Summary: "The Netherlands men's team has been an international soccer force for more than one hundred years, and the women's team is rising. With passionate fans and powerful players, the Netherlands teams have never been stronger"— Provided by publisher.
Identifiers: LCCN 2025016999 | ISBN 979-8-7656-8941-7 lib. bdg. | ISBN 979-8-3480-2933-3 pbk. | ISBN 979-8-7656-9874-7 epub
Subjects: LCSH: Nederlands Voetbalelftal (Soccer team)—Juvenile literature | National Women's Soccer League—Netherlands—Juvenile literature | Champions League (Soccer tournament) | World Cup (Soccer) | Soccer fans—Netherlands—Juvenile literature | Soccer—Netherlands—History—Juvenile literature

Classification: LCC GV944.N4 S35 2026 | DDC 796.33409492—dc23/eng/20250806
LC record available at https://lccn.loc.gov/2025016999

Manufactured in the United States of America
1-1012739-54809-8/11/2025

TABLE OF CONTENTS

Johan Cruyff (*left*) keeps his eyes on the ball during the 1974 Men's World Cup quarterfinals.

INTRODUCTION

A LEAD IN MINUTES

It was less than two minutes into the 1974 Men's World Cup final. The Netherlands was in complete control. They had yet to give up the ball to their opponent, West Germany. The Netherlands superstar midfielder Johan

Cruyff made his way toward the goal, but he was fouled by a West German player.

The referee blew his whistle. The Netherlands received a penalty kick. Midfielder Johan Neeskens stepped up to take the kick. He struck the ball straight down the center of the net.

Goal! The Netherlands was up 1–0 within minutes of their first ever Men's World Cup final. Although they ended up losing the match, many people think the 1974 men's team was the Netherlands' best national team ever.

FAST FACTS

The Netherlands men's national team nickname is the Orange, and the women's team nickname is the Orange Lionesses.

The 1974 men's national team played Total Football during the World Cup.

The Orange won the 1988 Union of European Football Associations (UEFA) European Championship title.

The Orange Lionesses won the 2017 UEFA European Women's Championship title.

Daniëlle van de Donk kicks the ball in a 2023 match against Belgium.

National soccer teams are made up of the country's most talented players. The biggest title to win is the World Cup. This event is organized by FIFA. Different countries host the event every four years.

The Netherlands also competes in the Summer Olympics. It is held every four years. The teams also play in the UEFA European Championship and the UEFA European Women's Championship every four years. Whether playing at home or away, the Netherlands national teams and fans are proud to be a sea of orange!

Netherlands fans wearing orange cheer on their favorite team in 2010.

The Orange at the 1912 Olympics

CHAPTER 1

ORANGE AND ORANGE LIONESSES

The Netherlands men's national soccer team is nicknamed the Orange. The Orange played their first game in 1905 against Belgium. The Netherlands won the game 4–1 in extra time. The team's first major wins happened at the 1908, 1912, and 1920 Olympic Games. At all three Olympics, the Orange won the bronze medal.

The Netherlands played in the Men's World Cup for the first time in 1934. But they lost to Switzerland in the first round. Four years later, the team once again lost in the first round, this time falling to Czechoslovakia. After this loss, it would be another 36 years before the Netherlands would qualify for another World Cup.

The Orange face Switzerland in the first round of the 1934 Men's World Cup.

At the Men's World Cup in 1974, the Orange were much more successful. Under the leadership of coach Rinus Michels and team captain Johan Cruyff, the Netherlands was unstoppable. They knocked out all of their opponents to advance to the final.

Rinus Michels (*center*) coaching the Orange at the 1974 World Cup final

The Orange at the 1974 World Cup final

The Orange faced West Germany in the Netherlands' first Men's World Cup final match. The game was played on their opponent's home turf in Munich. The Orange fought hard, but they ended up losing the game 2–1.

The Orange's style of play during this match was called Total Football. This style of play allows players to switch between different positions at any time on the field. Even though the Orange came up short of the top prize, their style of play proved to be a success.

The team made it to the Men's World Cup final again in 1978 and 2010 but came up short both times. Their best victory was in 1988 when they won the UEFA European Championship title against the Soviet Union. The Soviet Union was a nation that broke up into fifteen countries, including Russia, in 1991.

Marco van Basten runs with the ball in a match against England at the 1988 UEFA European Championship.

Annemieke Griffioen (*left*) fights for the ball in a 1999 match against the United States.

The Netherlands women's national soccer team is nicknamed the Orange Lionesses. They played their first match in 1973 against England. The team has been getting better and better since then. With the start of women's pro leagues in the Netherlands, women have the chance to play at high levels.

In 2009, the Orange Lionesses played in the UEFA European Women's Championship tournament for the first time. They made it to the semifinals. But they lost to England 2–1 and finished in third place. In 2015, the team played in its first Women's World Cup. They lost to Japan before the quarterfinals.

The Orange Lionesses's greatest victory was in 2017 when the team won the UEFA European Women's

The Orange Lionesses celebrate a goal during the semifinals of the 2009 UEFA European Women's Championship.

The Orange Lionesses celebrate winning the 2017 UEFA European Women's Championship.

Championship title. Coach Sarina Wiegman and team captains Sherida Spitse and Mandy van den Berg led the team to a 4–2 win against Denmark. Two years later, the Netherlands made it to the Women's World Cup final match. They finished second to the United States.

FROM PLAYER TO COACH

Sarina Wiegman was an Orange Lionesses midfielder before becoming the team's head coach. She was named FIFA's Best Women's Coach four times.

Rob Rensenbrink (*center*) controls the ball during the final of the Men's World Cup in 1978.

CHAPTER 2

EURO CHAMPIONS

The Netherlands men's national soccer team has played in the World Cup 11 times. They came close to winning the title three times. They finished second in 1974, 1978, and 2010. To reach the final in 1974, the Orange scored 14 total goals and allowed only one in the tournament.

Four years later, the Orange made it to the Men's World Cup final again. Forward Rob Rensenbrink had a chance to score and win the game. But his shot just missed and bounced off the goalpost. Argentina won 3–1.

The team had great success at the 1988 UEFA European Championship. In an early match against England, Marco van Basten of the Orange scored a hat trick to win the game. In the final, van Basten received a pass from teammate Robert Mühren and struck a volley into the back of the net. Goal! The strong play by van Basten and Mühren helped the Netherlands win the final.

Marco van Basten celebrates the Orange winning the 1988 UEFA European Championship.

WHOLE BODY SCORER

Robin van Persie made Men's World Cup history in 2014. He was the first player since 1966 to score goals in five different ways. He scored with his left foot, right foot, and head. He also scored on a free kick and penalty kick.

One of the greatest athletes to ever play for the Orange was Robin van Persie. He made his first appearance with the team in 2005. In 12 years of wearing the Orange jersey, van Persie logged 50 goals. This made him the all-time leading scorer for the team.

Robin van Persie (*right*) scores a goal during a qualifying match for the 2016 UEFA European Championship.

In 2010, the Orange were in a close Men's World Cup semifinal game against Uruguay. In the 18th minute of play, the Netherlands captain Giovanni van Bronckhorst got the ball. He took a shot from about 40 yards (36 m) away from the goal and scored. The Orange went on to win the game 3–2. But they lost to Spain in the final match.

The Netherlands women's team has played in three Women's World Cups. They played in the tournament for the first time in 2015. In a match against New Zealand, Lieke Martens took a shot in the 33rd minute of play. The ball soared toward the goal and into the right side of the net. Martens had just scored the team's first Women's World Cup goal. The team later lost to Japan.

Lieke Martens (*right*) passes the ball in a match against Canada at the 2015 Women's World Cup.

In 2017, the Orange Lionesses competed at the UEFA European Women's Championship. The team faced Denmark in the final. Early in the match, Denmark scored the first goal to take the lead. Minutes later, Vivianne Miedema scored for the Netherlands to tie the game.

Vivianne Miedema (*right*) playing in the final match of the 2017 UEFA European Women's Championship

Sherida Spitse (*left*) celebrates after scoring a goal in the final match against Denmark at the UEFA European Women's Championship in 2017.

A goal by Martens gave the Netherlands a 2–1 lead. But this was answered by another goal from Denmark. The hard-fought battle continued. A goal by midfielder Sherida Spitse and another from Miedema earned the Netherlands a 4–2 win. It was their first UEFA European Women's Championship title.

In 2019, the Orange Lionesses played in the Women's World Cup semifinals against Sweden. The game went to extra time. In the 99th minute of play, Netherlands midfielder Jackie Groenen took a shot and scored. The team moved on to the final match but lost to the US. Four years later, the Netherlands lost in a quarterfinal match against Spain.

In the 2024 UEFA European Championship, the Orange made it to the semifinal match. They were led by team captain Virgil van Dijk. Many people say van Dijk is the best defender in the world.

Left to right: **Crystal Dunn and Megan Rapinoe of the United States fight Desiree van Lunteren and Daniëlle van de Donk of the Netherlands for the ball during the 2019 Women's World Cup final.**

Netherlands fans gather for a parade in 2024.

CHAPTER 3

SEA OF ORANGE

The Netherlands is a small country. But the Orange and Orange Lionesses have many fans, known as the sea of orange. Both the men's and women's teams have won the hearts of soccer fans from their home country and from around the world.

WHY ORANGE?

The Netherlands national men's and women's soccer teams wear bright orange jerseys because it is the color of the Dutch royal family, the House of Orange-Nassau.

You don't need a close connection to the Netherlands to cheer for the Orange and Orange Lionesses. Their history of success and superstar players help make them popular. Fans from all around the world show up to cheer on the Netherlands no matter where the teams play.

Johan Cryuff Arena in 2023

Fans cheer on the Orange Lionesses during the final match of the 2019 Women's World Cup.

The sea of orange packs stadiums in the Netherlands for home games. Johan Cruyff Arena in Amsterdam can host around 55,000 fans. During tournaments, fans hold orange parades. Fans wear orange and march together to the stadium. The dancing, chanting, and cheering continue in the stadium long after kickoff.

Daniëlle van de Donk (*top*) and Kerstin Casparij (*bottom*) celebrate an Orange Lionesses goal during a 2023 match.

Since the Orange Lionesses won the 2017 UEFA European Women's Championship, the team has gained more interest and support. Fans can tune in for both the Orange Lionesses and Orange as they compete in soccer's biggest events.

The sea of orange support their teams at soccer's biggest events.

NETHERLANDS MEN'S SOCCER TIMELINE

1905 The Netherlands plays its first official match against Belgium.

1908 The Orange win their first Olympic bronze medal.

1934 The Orange make their first Men's World Cup appearance.

1974 The Netherlands finishes second in the Men's World Cup.

1978 The Netherlands finishes second in the Men's World Cup.

1988 The Orange win the UEFA European Championship.

2010 They finish second in the Men's World Cup.

2022 They finish fifth in the Men's World Cup.

NETHERLANDS WOMEN'S SOCCER TIMELINE

1973 The Orange Lionesses play their first official match against England.

2009 They make their first appearance in the UEFA European Women's Championship and finish third.

2015 The Orange Lionesses make their first Women's World Cup appearance.

2017 The Netherlands wins its first UEFA European Women's Championship.

2019 The Netherlands finishes second at the Women's World Cup.

2020 They play in the Olympics for the first time.

2022 The Orange Lionesses play in a quarterfinal game of the UEFA European Women's Championship.

2023 The Orange Lionesses play in a quarterfinal game of the Women's World Cup.

GLOSSARY

extra time: time added to the end of a soccer game

FIFA: the group that oversees soccer around the world

goalpost: one of the two vertical supports holding up the crossbar of a soccer goal

hat trick: three goals scored in a game by one person

midfielder: a player who usually stays in the middle of the field between the forwards and the defenders

penalty kick: a free kick at the goal allowed for certain fouls or to decide the winner of some games

quarterfinal: a game or series of games to determine the final four teams or athletes in a tournament

semifinal: a game or series of games coming before the final round in a tournament

Total Football: a strategy of play where players change positions to attack and defend

UEFA European Championship: a tournament that happens every four years and determines the best national team in Europe

volley: a kick of the ball while it is in the air

LEARN MORE

Goldstein, Margaret J. *Women's Professional Soccer.* Lerner Publications, 2026.

Kiddle: Netherlands National Football Team Facts for Kids
https://kids.kiddle.co/Netherlands_national_football_team

KNVB: Men's National Team
https://www.knvb.com/oranje/mens-national-team

KNVB: Women's National Team
https://www.knvb.com/oranje/womens-national-team

Lowe, Alexander. *G.O.A.T. Soccer Strikers.* Lerner Publications, 2022.

Shaw, Gina. *What Is the Women's World Cup?* Penguin Workshop, 2023.

INDEX

PHOTO ACKNOWLEDGMENTS

Image credits: STF/Getty Images, p. 4; GERRIT VAN KEULEN/Getty Images, p. 6; Frans Lemmens/Alamy, pp. 7, 27; Bob Thomas/Popperfoto/Getty Images, pp. 8, 10–11; Keystone-France/Getty Images, p. 9; Leo Mason/Popperfoto/Getty Images, p. 12; Tom Hauck/Getty Images, p. 13; Ian Walton/Getty Images, p. 14; Anadolu/Getty Images, pp. 15, 20; VI-Images/Getty Images, p. 16; Bongarts/Getty Images, p. 17; Dean Mouhtaropoulos/Getty Images, p. 18; Minas Panagiotakis/Getty Images, p. 19; TOBIAS SCHWARZ/Getty Images, p. 21; Maja Hitij/Getty Images, p. 22; Soccrates Images/Getty Images, pp. 23, 26; Milos Ruzicka/Getty Images, p. 24; Romain Biard/Shutterstock, p. 25. Design elements: Ralf Hiemisch/Getty Images; Rifqyhsn Design/Getty Images; cunfek/Getty Images; poo worawit/Getty Images.

Cover: Andrew Milligan/Press Association via AP Images (left); Marcel van Dorst/EYE4images/NurPhoto via AP (right).